For

Mason Rhea

From

Mimi & Papa

Happy Easter

Date _____

my little Prayers

Illustrations by
Stephanie McFetridge Britt
Compiled by Brenda Ward

A Division of Thomas Nelson Publishers
Since 1798

www.thomasnelson.com

MY LITTLE PRAYERS
Copyright © 1993 by Tommy Nelson®, a Division of Thomas
Nelson, Inc.
Illustrations copyright © 1993 by Stephanie Britt.

All rights reserved. No portion of this book may be reproduced
in any form without the written permission of the publisher,
with the exception of brief excerpts in reviews.

The publisher has made every effort to locate the owners of all
copyrighted material and to obtain permission to reprint the
prayers in this book. Any errors are unintentional, and correc-
tions will be made in future editions if necessary. The publishers acknowledge special thanks for the permission received
from the following:

Celebration for "The Butterfly Song" by Brian Howard, copyright © 1974, 1975 by Celebration. "A Great Gray Elephant"
courtesy of the National Society to Prevent Blindness.
"Sometimes by Step" by Rich Mullins, copyright © 1992 BMG
Songs, Inc./Kid Brothers of St. Frank Publishing.

Published in Nashville, Tennessee, by Tommy Nelson®, a
Division of Thomas Nelson, Inc. Visit us on the Web at
www.tommynelson.com.

Scripture quotations identified ICB are from the *International
Children's Bible*®, *New Century Version*®, copyright © 1986,
1988, 1999 by Tommy Nelson®, a Division of Thomas Nelson,
Inc. Entries marked KJV are from the King James Version.

ISBN 10: 1-4003-0648-5 (2005 edition)
ISBN 13: 978-1-4003-0648-0 (2005 edition)
ISBN: 0-8499-1064-1
Printed in China
07 08 09 LEO 9 8 7 6

Contents

The Lord is all I need.
He takes care of me.

PSALM 16:5

MY DAY

Day by day, dear Lord, of Thee
Three things I pray:
To see Thee more clearly,
Love Thee more dearly,
Follow Thee more nearly,
Day by day.

St. Richard of Chichester

Oh God, You are my God,
And I will ever praise You.
I will seek You in the morning,
And I will learn to walk in Your
ways.
And step by step You'll lead me,
And I will follow You all of my
days.

Rich Mullins

For this new morning with its light,
For rest and shelter of the night,
For health and food,
For love and friends,
For every gift Your goodness sends,
We thank You, gracious Lord. Amen.

Traditional

All for You, dear
  God.
Everything I do,
Or think,
Or say,
The whole day long.
Help me to be good.

Unknown

When the weather is wet,
We must not fret.
When the weather is cold,
We must not scold.
When the weather is warm,
We must not storm...
Be thankful together,
Whatever the weather.

Unknown

He gives food to every living creature.
His love continues forever.

PSALM 136:25

MY MEALTIME

God is great.
God is good.
Let us thank Him
for our food.

Traditional

Thank you for the world so sweet,
Thank you for the food we eat,
Thank you for the birds that sing,
Thank you, God, for everything!

E. Rutter Leatham

The Lord is good to me,
and so I thank the Lord.
For giving me the things I need:
the sun, the rain, and the
apple seed!
The Lord is good to me.

Traditional

God, we thank you for this food,
For rest and home and all things
   good;
For wind and rain and sun above,
But most of all for those we love.

Maryleona Frost

I go to bed and sleep in peace.
Lord, only you keep me safe.

PSALM 4:8

My Bedtime

Now I lay me down to sleep.
I pray Thee, Lord, my soul to keep.
Your love be with me through
the night
And wake me with the morning
light.

Traditional

Lord, keep us safe this night,
Secure from all our fears.
May angels guard us while we sleep,
Till morning light appears.

Traditional

ord, with Your praise we drop off
to sleep.
Carry us through the night,
Make us fresh for the morning.
Hallelujah for the day!
And blessing for the night!

from a Ghanaian fisherman's prayer

Father, we thank You for the night,
And for the pleasant morning light,
For rest and food and loving care,
And all that makes the day so fair.

Help us to do the things we should,
To be to others kind and good;
In all we do and all we say,
To grow more loving every day.

Unknown

Children, obey your parents the way the Lord wants. This is the right thing to do.

EPHESIANS 6:1

My Family
and
Friends

God bless all those that I love.
God bless all those that love me.
God bless all those that love
those that I love, and all those
that love those who love me.

New England Sampler

Thank You for my parents, Lord,
and all the fun we've had.
There's no time I love better
than with my mom and dad.

Help me, Lord, to always know
the many ways they care.
For toys and snacks and big bear hugs
and always being there.

When I grow up, I want to be
just like my parents, too.
Because they make me feel so great
and love me just like You.

Beth Burt

42

May the road rise to meet you,
May the wind be always at your
 back,
May the sun shine warm on your
 face,
The rain fall softly on your fields;
And until we meet again,
May God hold you in the palm of
 His hand.

Traditional, Irish

Dear Lord,

Thank You for my grandparents.

They always have time to read to
me or play games.

They like to tickle and play and
laugh.

And they like ice cream and going
to the park, too.

Mostly though, God, they love me.

Please take care of them, Lord.

I think they must be a lot like You.

Anonymous

Our family's big, our
   house is small;
We're crowded as can be.
But, Father, there's a lot of love
That's shared here happily.

I love my mom and daddy, too;
They keep me safe each day.
But thanks for brothers and sisters,
   Lord;
They have more time to play.

Mary Hollingsworth

The Lord is my shepherd.
I have everything I need.

PSALM 23:1

My Favorite Things

Please give me what I ask,
   dear Lord,
If You'd be glad about it.
But if You think it's not for me,
Please help me do without it.

Traditional

Dear Father,
Hear and bless
Thy beasts and singing birds.
And guard with tenderness
Small things that have no
words.

Unknown

A great gray elephant,
A little yellow bee,
A tiny purple violet,
A tall green tree,
A red and white sailboat
On a blue sea—
All these things
You gave to me,
When you made
My eyes to see—
Thank You, God.

*National Society for the
Prevention of Blindness, Inc.*

If I were a butterfly,
I'd thank You, Lord, for giving me
   wings,
And if I were a robin in a tree,
I'd thank You, Lord, that I could
   sing,
And if I were a fish in the sea,
I'd wiggle my tail, and I'd giggle
   with glee,
But I just thank You, Father,
   for making me *me*.

Brian Howard

When I am afraid,
I will trust you.

PSALM 56:3

My Feelings

Dear Lord,
Thank you that I am sometimes
    strong,
    help me when I am still weak;
Thank you that I am sometimes wise,
    help me when I am still foolish;
Thank you that I have sometimes
    done well,
    forgive me the times I have failed
    You;
And teach me to serve You and Your
    world
    with love and faith and truth,
    with hope and grace and good
    humor. Amen

A Swaledale Parish Prayer

I feel happy, Jesus!
I am happy when I laugh with
    friends, or hold a puppy.
I feel happy eating ice cream, or lis-
    tening to a story.
I feel happy when someone says,
    "I love you."
Lord, I am happy because I belong
    to You!
That is the best thing of all to be
    happy about!

Sheryl Crawford

Dear God, my friend is moving,
and I'm so sad.

We've had so much fun together,
and I don't want her to move.

Please help her to find new
friends where she's going so
she won't be lonely.

And help me to make new
friends, too.

Thank You, Jesus, for being my
best friend.

Anonymous

Dear God, be good to me.
The sea is so wide,
and my boat is so small.

The Breton Fisherman's Prayer

Jesus, someone I care for lives
with You now.
I feel very sad because that person
is not here.
Sometimes I cry... to let the sadness
out.
Lord, You say that people who
live with You are happy.
In heaven, there are angels and
friends and family.
Jesus, please help me to remember
that someday we will be together
again with the ones we love...
And we will live forever with
You in heaven!

Sheryl Crawford

This is the day that the Lord has made.
Let us rejoice and be glad today!

PSALM 118:24

My Special Days

My Birthday

Dear Lord, I am happy today
  because it is MY BIRTHDAY!
I was born on a day like today.
It was a great day for my family,
  one they could never forget.
Thank You for fun things,
  like cake and candles,
  for family and friends and
  presents and birthday cards.
But most of all, Lord, thank
  You for giving me life!

Sheryl Crawford

Christmas

What can I give Him,
Poor as I am?
If I were a shepherd,
I would bring Him a lamb.
If I were a wise man,
I would do my part.
But what can I give Him?
Give Him my heart.

Christina G. Rossetti

Christmas

Away in a manger, no crib for a bed,
The little Lord Jesus laid down
   His sweet head;
The stars in the sky looked
   down where He lay,
The little Lord Jesus, asleep on the hay.
Be near me, Lord Jesus; I ask
   Thee to stay
Close by me for ever, and love me,
   I pray;
Bless all the dear children in
   Thy tender care,
Prepare us for heaven, to live
   with Thee there.

Martin Luther

Easter

He is Lord,
He is Lord!
He is risen from the dead
  and He is Lord!
Every knee shall bow;
Every tongue confess,
that Jesus Christ is Lord.

Traditional

The Lord listens when I pray
to him.

PSALM 4:3

My Time With God

Two little eyes to look to God;
Two little ears to hear His word;
Two little feet to walk in His ways;
Two little lips to sing His praise;
Two little hands to do His will;
And one little heart to love Him still.

Traditional

All things bright and
  beautiful,
All creatures great and small,
All things wise and wonderful,
The Lord God made them all.

He gave us eyes to see them,
And lips that we might tell
How great is God Almighty,
Who has made all things well!

Carl Frances Alexander

God be in my head
And in my understanding.
God be in mine eyes
And in my looking.
God be in my mouth
And in my speaking.
God be in my heart
And in my thinking.

Unknown

The Lord's Prayer

Our Father which art in heaven
Hallowed be thy name.
Thy kingdom come.
Thy will be done
   in earth, as it is in heaven.
Give us this day our daily bread.
And forgive us our trespasses,
As we forgive those who trespass
   against us.
And lead us not into temptation,
But deliver us from evil:
For thine is the kingdom,
And the power, and the glory,
For ever. Amen.

Matthew 6:9–13, KJV

Stephanie McFetridge Britt is a freelance illustrator for books, greeting cards, and magazines. She has illustrated over 30 children's books. Prior to her freelance work, Britt worked six years for Hallmark Cards, Inc. She and her husband live in Hawaii.